D1765244

Nothing I Never Done

Peter Leigh

Published in association with
The Basic Skills Agency

Hodder & Stoughton

A MEMBER OF THE HODDER HEADLINE GROUP

Acknowledgements
Cover: Nanette Hoogslag

Orders: please contact Bookpoint Ltd, 130 Milton Park, Abingdon, Oxon OX14
4SB. Telephone: (44) 01235 827720, Fax: (44) 01235 400454. Lines are open from
9.00–6.00, Monday to Saturday, with a 24 hour message answering service.

Cataloguing in Publication Data is available from the British Library.

ISBN 0 340 86954 2

First published 1997
This edition published 2002
Impression number   10 9 8 7 6 5 4 3 2 1
Year   2007 2006 2005 2004 2003 2002

Typeset by Fakenham Photosetting Ltd, Fakenham, Norfolk.
Printed in Great Britain for Hodder & Stoughton Educational, a division of
Hodder Headline Plc, 338 Euston Road, London NW1 3BH by Athenaeum Press
Ltd, Gateshead, Tyne & Wear.

About the play

The People
- Raj
- Gary

The Place
The school bike sheds.

What's Happening
Gary skids his bike round the corner,
and stops by his place.
Raj is already there.
He is locking his bike up.
Gary pushes his bike up into the rack.

Act 1

Gary	You going down the club tonight?
Raj	The club?
Gary	Yes.
Raj	No, I hate the club.
Gary	You were there last night!
Raj	I know! I go there, but I still hate it.
Gary	Why do you go if you hate it?
Raj	It's that Larry.
Gary	Larry?
Raj	Yeah, Larry. The one that runs it. I hate him.
Gary	What's wrong with Larry?
Raj	I don't know! I just hate him.
Gary	Why?
Raj	I just said, I don't know!

I don't know why I hate him.

Gary   You can't just hate someone for no reason.

Raj   Well, I can. I hate Larry.

Gary   That's silly! You've got to have a reason.

Raj   No, you don't! You hate that girl, don't you?

Gary   What girl?

Raj   The one that beat you up.
That Mandy.

Gary   She didn't beat me up.
No girl ever beat me up.

Raj   Yes she did. You wanted a lick of her ice-cream, and she wouldn't give you one.

Gary   So?

Raj   And you kept going on at her, and

hanging round her, and pestering
her, and in the end she got fed up,
and stuffed the ice-cream
in your face.

Gary   So?

Raj   She held you down, and wiped the
ice-cream all round your face.

Gary   So?

Raj   And then got her friends to come
and lick it off.

Gary   Yes, but she still didn't beat me up.

Raj   Well, her.

Gary   What about her?

Raj   Well you hate her don't you?
And you've got no reason.
Well it's just the same with Larry.
I hate him. That's all.
I always have done.

(Pause)

	Ever since he threw me out.
Gary	He threw you out?
Raj	Yes, he was great until then.
	And then one night,
	last night in fact,
	he just threw me out.
	Just like that. For no reason.
Gary	For no reason?
Raj	Well, there was this little rip on the
	pool table. A little tiny rip!
	It was only a few centimetres long.
	Well perhaps a bit more.
	In fact it was more like half a metre.
	But it wasn't my fault.
	I didn't even do it!
	It was Jon-Paul.

Gary	Jon-Paul?
Raj	Yes! The big show off! He was showing off to everybody about how he could do this trick with the cue ball. Make it jump in the air.
Gary	Jump in the air?
Raj	Yes! The big show off!
Gary	And what were you doing?
Raj	I was standing behind him with the other cue.
Gary	What happened?
Raj	Well, he bent over the table to make his shot.
Gary	Yes?
Raj	Well, as he made his shot to make the cue ball jump in the air, I made my shot.

Gary And?

Raj I made him jump in the air!

Gary You mean you stuck your cue up
his . . . ?

Raj Yes!

Gary What happened?

Raj He jerked up, and ripped the cloth
on the pool table.

Gary So Jon-Paul ripped it!

Raj   Yes! If he hadn't have jerked,
he would never have ripped it.
But Larry blamed me.
As if it was my fault.
And then he threw me out.
For no reason.

Gary   Just for that? For a little nick on
the pool table? He threw you out?

Raj   Yes. Just for that!

*Gary finishes locking his bike, and
starts to pack his bag.
Raj slings his bag over his shoulder.*

Raj   Mind you, there was the cue!

Gary   The cue?

Raj   When Jon-Paul ripped the cloth,
everybody was laughing at him.

And he got really mad.
I don't know why.
It was only a joke.
But he threw a real wobbler.
And I only gave him a little prod.

Gary He always did have a bad temper,
that Jon-Paul.

Raj Exactly!
Well, he gets all mad, and then he
has a go at me.

Gary No?

Raj Yes! For no reason at all!
He gets his pool cue, and swipes it
at me.

Gary Did he hit you?

Raj No. I ducked.
He hit the wall instead.

Gary	And the cue . . . ?
Raj	Broke!
Gary	So, just for that,
	Larry threw you out?
Raj	Just for that!
	Just because Jon-Paul lost his
	temper, and ripped
	his precious pool table,
	and broke his precious cue,
	he threw me out.
Gary	It's not fair!
Raj	I know! It wasn't my fault.

They brood in silence.

Raj	*(after a while)*
	Mind you, there were the cups.
Gary	The cups?

Raj Yes. And the saucers . . . and the coffee . . . and the tea . . . and the milk and the sugar.

Gary The saucers, the coffee, the tea, and the milk and the sugar?

Raj Yes . . . and the carpet!

Gary The carpet?

Raj Yes, but that was Jon-Paul's fault as well.
If he hadn't have got out of the way, everything would have been all right.

Gary He got out of the way?

Raj Well after Jon-Paul had a go at me with the snooker cue,
I got a bit angry.

Gary Well, anyone would.
Being attacked like that.

Raj	Of course they would.
	Stands to reason.
	Well I got a bit angry, and threw
	my cue at him.
Gary	Did it hit him?
Raj	No, he ducked as well.
Gary	What happened to the cue?
Raj	Well, you know that little snack bar
	that's in the club?
Gary	The one where they put the cups
	and the saucers?
Raj	Yes, that one.
Gary	And the coffee, and the tea, and the
	milk and the sugar?
Raj	Yes. Well, Jon-Paul was standing in
	front of that.
Gary	And . . . ?
Raj	Well, when the cue missed

Jon-Paul, it hit that!

Gary And the cups and the saucers and the milk and the sugar and the coffee and the tea . . .

Raj . . . were all knocked off . . .

Gary . . . on to the carpet!

Raj Right!

Gary I see!

Raj And so Larry blames me!
As if it's my fault!
As if I wanted to break all those cups and saucers and things.
I couldn't help it.
It was Jon-Paul, ducking out of the way like that.
If it's anyone's fault, it's his.
But Larry blamed me. He's always picking on me. And he threw me out.

	So that's why I hate him.
	And that's why I'm not going to the club.
Gary	Oh. I see.
Raj	*(brightening up)*
	But we could go to the centre.
Gary	The centre?
Raj	Yes! Let's go there instead.
Gary	I can't go to the centre.
Raj	Why not?
Gary	I got thrown out last night.
	For no reason at all.
	Just because of a silly little bin.
	I ask you . . .

But the bell rings, and they go into school.

Act 2

The end of lunchtime.
Raj *is in the bike sheds, checking his bike.*
Gary *comes running up.*
He looks excited.

Gary   You know that Jon-Paul?

Raj   What about him?

Gary   I've just seen him, and he says he's
going to get you.

Raj   He's going to get me?

Gary   He says he's going to get you for
showing him up at the club.
He says he's going to stuff your
teeth so far down your throat,

	you'll be eating your own breakfast.
Raj	He said that?
Gary	He said that after he's finished you'll need a passport so people can recognise you.
Raj	Will I?
Gary	And he gave me 10p to start the collection for your funeral.
Raj	*(looking a little pale)* Do you think he was joking?
Gary	Joking? No, I don't think he was joking.
Raj	*(throwing his chest out)* Well, I'd like to see him try, that's all.
Gary	He is big.
Raj	Size doesn't matter.
Gary	And strong.

Raj	Strength isn't everything.
Gary	And he does do karate, and kung-fu, and he is a black belt at judo.
Raj	Look, none of them things matter. In a fight there's only one thing that matters.
Gary	And what's that then?
Raj	Brains. You've got to have them up here.

Raj taps the side of his head.

Gary	That's you finished then!
Raj	Look, you don't have to worry about me. I can look after myself. I'll be ready, any time he comes.
Gary	That's good because he's coming after school.

Raj	After school?
Gary	Yes. Behind the bike sheds.
	I said you'd be there.
Raj	Oh, thanks!
Gary	Well, what are friends for?
	I said you'd be ready for him.
	I said you'd always hated him.
	I said you thought he was a big prat.
	I said you couldn't wait
	to do him over.
	I said you were going to break his
	arms, and his legs.
	I said you were going to shove his
	face where his bum should be.
Raj	You said all that?
Gary	Yes. And that you were going to
	tie him up in his own black belt.

	And stuff him in the bin where he
	belonged.
Raj	Thanks a lot!
Gary	That's all right. Anything to help.
Raj	Look, you know you said he'd be
	coming after school.
Gary	Yes?
Raj	Well I just remembered.
	I've got a detention after school.

Gary	A detention?
Raj	Old Smithy gave me a detention.
Gary	You've had lots of detentions.
Raj	I know.
Gary	And you've never been to one of them.
Raj	Well, that's why I've got to go to this one.
	Otherwise I'll be in real trouble!
Gary	Well that's all right.
	The detention will only last ten minutes.
	We'll wait till you've finished.
Raj	Oh no!
	This one's going on for hours and hours, because I've missed all the others.
	I won't get out until five o'clock . . .

Six o'clock . . . In fact it probably
won't be until seven
that I get out.

Gary You're not trying to chicken out of
this, are you?

Raj What, me? (*Raj sounds shocked*)
Course not! You know me.
I'm not scared of anything.
No, it's just that if I don't do this
detention I'll get expelled.

Gary Well, what about tomorrow?

Raj I'm going out with my Mum.

Gary The day after?

Raj I'm going out with my Dad.

Gary The day after that?

Raj I'm going out with my cousin.

Gary But I've told Jon-Paul you'll be
waiting for him.

Raj	Well, you'll just have tell him I'm sorry.
	It's not that I don't want to.
	I'm dead keen.
	I want to get in there,
	and bash his brains out,
	and do him over, but I just can't
	manage it this week,
	and probably not next week neither.
Gary	Why can't you tell him yourself?
Raj	Well, I would do, but I can't.
	I'm nipping off home early before he
	sees me.

Raj jumps on his bike, and pedals off.

Act 3

After school in the bike sheds.
Raj is still there.
Gary comes in, and is surprised to see him.

Gary   Hey! I thought you were going home.

Raj   I was, but then I got caught at the gates,
and sent back.

Gary   Well, you better get a move on now,
because Jon-Paul will be here soon.

Raj   That doesn't worry me.

Gary   What? Even though he said
he'll kill you, and stuff your teeth
down your throat?

Raj   No!

Gary   Even though he's bigger than you
and stronger than you
and does karate and kung-fu
and has got a black belt in judo?

Raj   No!

Gary   You're not scared at all?
Not even one tiny little bit?

Raj   No! Not even one tiny little bit!
And I'll tell you why. Because it's
not me that needs to be scared.
It's a so-called friend of mine that
needs to be scared.

Gary   What do you mean?

Raj   Well, I saw Jon-Paul just now in the
boys' toilets.
And he said he wasn't mad at me at
all after last night.

He thought it was a great laugh.
All those coffee-cups and milk
going everywhere.
At least he wasn't mad until he met this
friend of mine.

Gary (*nervously*)
A friend of yours?

Raj That's what I said.

Well, this friend started stirring,
and getting Jon-Paul riled.
He kept saying that I was going round
saying what a prat Jon-Paul was, and
how I was going to smash his face in.
And how I was looking for him, and
how big I was,
and how strong I was, and how I did
karate and kung-fu and had a black belt
in judo.

Gary   Oh!

Raj   Which friend of mine would say
something like that do you think?

Gary   I've no idea!

Raj   Nor have I! Well anyway, after me and
Jon-Paul had talked for a bit, and found
out that we weren't mad at each other.

We decided that this so-called friend
needed teaching a lesson.

Gary   *(shakily)*
A lesson?

Raj   Yes! A good, hard lesson!
For stirring things up.
So we decided we'd meet here after
school, find out who it was, and do
him over good and proper.

Gary   Oh!

Raj   In fact Jon-Paul should be along
any minute now.

Gary   *(fumbling with his bike)*
Well I think I better be off now.

Raj   Don't you want to see the fight.

Gary   No, I can't stop.

He pulls his bike out of the rack.

Raj   Don't you want to find out who this so-called friend is?

Gary   No . . . really! I've got to go! I've . . . er . . . I've . . .

Raj   I think I can hear Jon-Paul now.

Gary   Bye!

Gary rides off.
He doesn't do any skids or jumps.
He just pedals very fast.